BEHIND CLOSED DOORS

Henry Turnbull

BEHIND CLOSED DOORS

Henry Turnbull

malcolm down
PUBLISHING

First published 2020 by Malcolm Down Publishing Ltd.
www.malcolmdown.co.uk

24 23 22 21 20   7 6 5 4 3 2 1

British Library Cataloguing in Publication Data
A catalogue record for this book is available from the British Library.

ISBN 978-1-912863-51-8

Cover design by Esther Kotecha
Art direction by Sarah Grace

Printed in the UK

Some names have been changed to protect identities.

Contents

Acknowledgements

All my love and thanks to Alex, Alice, Bob, Charlie, Dave, David, Fiona, Jake, Jessie, Jonah, Megane, Matt, Max, Sarah, both Simons and Zara. You all gave so much care, support and input into this book at a moment's notice, which will never be forgotten!

Foreword

I first met Henry as a bright, active thirteen-year-old boy in our youth ministry, and getting to watch him grow from that boy into the man he is today I count as one of the biggest privileges of my life. The man Henry has grown into is marked by his humility, his love for those around him, and his love for and obedience to God. It's no surprise, then, that at its heart, this book too is drenched in humility, a love for those who read it and with a love for God and a desire to follow Him.

If you're a teenager and you've picked up this book – read it. I promise it will be worth it. It will show you that you are not alone in a pornography addiction, that God loves you and wants to set you free, and you'll find steps to help you travel towards that God-given freedom. Even if porn and masturbation are not a battle for you, *Behind Closed Doors* will help you to help your friends.

If you're a youth leader like myself, this book will give you an excellent framework for opening the tricky conversation about pornography and masturbation with your young people. For me, reading in the first few chapters about how many of my former young people were struggling with pornography was heart-breaking. It's been an important reminder to me that we need to actively create safe spaces for young people to be honest if they are struggling. *Behind Closed Doors* is a brilliant interactive resource not only for young people to read themselves, but also as a framework to create easy and safe conversations in one-to-one mentoring and small groups.

Simon Tulett
Youth minister, Christ Church Chorleywood

About Me, the Author

I never liked school. It was boring. I wanted adventure, risk, adrenaline and excitement. I have always been driven to make the most of every day and fill my life with stories, memories, and with that attitude of 'just give it a go' forever pushing me.

I've always loved God too. Of course, I used to pray and ask Him to use me, but I never considered that might actually happen.

At a youth festival in 2014, at the age of fifteen, God met with me and told me about a specific purpose He had for my life. Although at the time I did not know the exact details of this plan, I ran from it, wanting to pursue my own future. I loved God, but I never thought of Christianity as a brutally exhilarating adventure. From an early age I had dreamed of a career in the military and chased nothing else. However, some unforeseen circumstances that arose aged seventeen shut the door to my military desires.

When my military dreams were crushed, I had to make a choice about where to go next in life. I knew that God was still waiting for me with a whole different career, calling and passion, but still I was not ready to give up everything to entirely embrace what God had for me.

I had left school at sixteen and was in college on a course that seemed like a waste of time. I dropped out when I was seventeen to pursue a career as a full-time firefighter. I tried, on multiple different occasions, to join the fire service; however, God kept calling to me to go after what He had for me.

Finally, after years of God pursuing me, I willingly surrendered to the call on my life and was baptised by my friends in the cold swell of Polzeath Beach, Cornwall. God ignited a passion in me to not only see people meet Jesus, but to see them find freedom through Christ from the burdens that hold us down in life. God is now leading me deeper into this calling and has also walked me through many challenges and has broken many chains that have held *me* down.

After a long battle with pornography, God freed me from that six-year addiction and inspired me to see a whole generation of young people freed from pornography addictions. *Behind Closed Doors* is my attempt to put down in words what God has done for me, and I hope it may reach others too. In this book, I really have found risk, adrenaline and excitement. It turns out following Jesus really is an adventure, and although I don't know what I'm doing, God does, so I thought I'd just give it a go.

Start Here

The two big words

Pornography and masturbation. These two words are uncomfortable even to say. Just thinking about those two words can make you feel gross and awkward. Unfortunately, the lack of conversation about this stuff – and this world, that throws it at us – has allowed for millions of people to find themselves addicted to it. And being a Christian does not exclude us from that possibility.

I wrote this book for those people. You're a Christian who's still in school or stepping into adult life and you find yourself addicted to pornography and masturbation. You want out of this mess you've found yourself in, but you're blind to know where to begin or how to end it.

In this book you'll find:

- Encouragement.
- A sense that you're not alone in this.
- Honesty from guys and girls who have lived or are living with this addiction.
- Ideas, action steps and advice that may help you.
- A noise that goes against the silence around the topic of pornography and masturbation.
- God-given truths about pornography, masturbation but most vitally, about you.

Pornography grips the lives of so many of us and damages everyone it can, but none are excluded from the freedom found in Jesus.

If you're ready to get real honest and real raw; if you're ready to ask yourself some hard-hitting questions and look deep within yourself; if you're ready to end this addiction; if you're ready to boldly approach the throne of God and ask for your chains to be cut – then keep reading.

Where This Began

Why am I qualified to talk about porn,
and why write a book at all?

I was just twelve years old when it happened, starting out in secondary school life. A favourite conversation for the boys at school was pornography and the discovery of masturbation. I was brought up in a Christian home and was curious to find out what the lads were on about. I never intended for it to go as far, or for it to become as challenging as it did; I just wanted to understand. However, no one told me that pornography is a hook, and just how easy it is to get dragged in. My young curiosity opened the door to one video which soon spiralled beyond my control. I had accidently stepped into a world of hell; it felt good but I knew it was bad, yet I couldn't get out. So that was that; at just twelve years of age I was addicted to online pornography.

Porn is like a drug, and I acted accordingly. I was always desperate for my next 'hit'. For six long years I would spend every waking moment agonisingly searching my brain for new genres I could search for, or ways of finding fresh porn. I wasted so much time viewing endless hours of it, each time venturing further and further into the vast world of porn, seeking out that next thrill that I really didn't want, but that I had to find. I was completely and utterly consumed by pornography. I could not think of anything else. For six years my mind, my emotions and my actions all evolved around porn. It seemed so sweet, so innocent, so harmless. And yet, I was out of control.

As the years went by, I was sucked deeper and deeper into the dark world of pornography. At the same time, as I grew older, my Christian faith grew stronger. I would help out with the kids' work on a Sunday morning at church, and youth group on a Tuesday. I started preaching and took up an internship with a Christian charity, all the while desperately seeking freedom from this snare of pornography that controlled my life behind closed doors.

No one at church ever spoke about anything like this. For this reason, I honestly believed that of my Christian friends and everyone in the youth group, I was the only one addicted to pornography and masturbation. I believed this until I was sixteen.

A friend and I had been walking to church and back each evening. We would just walk and talk, and they were chilled moments. After a year of this, however, the conversation dried up and we had run out of things to talk about. After a few paces in dead silence my friend saw his opportunity, plucked up the courage and said, 'Can I ask you something?'

Let's be honest, whenever anyone asks you that, it's always going to be serious. My heart began beating a little faster, all possible scenarios flooding my mind, and so I nervously replied, 'Sure.' But what he asked me, I never saw coming.

It takes courage, and I'm so thankful for his bravery, because this moment, right here with my friend, was the start of my long journey to freedom. He asked, 'As a Christian, what's your view on pornography?'

I had been chained to the addiction of pornography for four years and had managed to keep it hidden. My heart and my faith were burning for a way out of this addiction that controlled me. I was completely helpless in the situation that I had unintentionally brought upon myself years before. Yet I had no idea where to begin to find freedom. But through my friend having the guts to ask me that question, Jesus, and therefore freedom, found me.

I was taken on a long journey by the Lord in which He led me to my freedom. The conversation with my friend happened when I was sixteen, but it still took another two years before I was free.

I was confused as a teenager about where to even begin with this addiction. *What do I even do to try to fight it?* I felt overwhelmed with all the content, material and opinions on what I should or should not be doing. I just needed some love, some support and something I could put into practice to begin my fight against my addiction. I didn't need some long theological dissection of biblical writings with great in-depth teaching on this subject matter. I didn't have time for that. I didn't have the energy for that. I'm not even sure if I have the brain for that. I just needed somewhere to start; all of that other stuff could come later.

So that's what this is. This book is my attempt to quickly and simply put down in words what the Lord taught me to do to ground myself so I wasn't always being knocked back by this addiction. And possibly it might start you off on your own journey to freedom.

So, there I was, walking home from church with my friend who had just asked me my view on pornography. My lack of conversation about this, and the fear of judgement or embarrassment encouraged me to give a vague answer, avoid the question and quickly think of something else to talk about. However, I chose to open up in that moment, as terrifying as it was.

I told him I had been hooked and struggling with pornography since I was twelve. He then told me his story, which was just like mine. Somehow, he too had ended up in the trap of pornography and was looking for an escape, but didn't know how to go about that. We continued, forcing ourselves to be open, and we confessed everything.

I remember the feeling of not wanting the walk home to end because it felt so good to finally share my darkest secret with someone who was living with the same secret. I'm not sure how we got to this point, but by the time we were stood outside my house in the dark, we had sworn to support one another in our struggle and figure out how it was that we were going to get free.

The weeks went on and all we would talk about on our walks to church was our shared battle. We opened up more, and with every week we found it easier and easier to chat about pornography and masturbation until there was nothing too gross or too awkward to bring up.

From this point we tried to talk to our other friends who were Christians. Some admitted that they too were hooked on pornography; some weren't ready to talk, and some didn't think it was wrong. But out of those who wanted it, we formed a group of lads who were hooked on pornography and masturbation and wanted out. This group was our way of sharing, talking, looking after each other and fighting back against pornography. It was the start to many of us breaking free, or being the closest to freedom we'd ever been.

That's how it was for the next year; we helped each other to fight the temptation. One thing was common to us all – failure. Sometimes we would last a day without porn and then fall back into it. Sometimes we could go for a week and then fail. Sometimes we lasted a month, sometimes two months; each time we thought we were free, but we'd then fall back. I remember going four months without pornography and I thought that was it, I was free. I remember sitting on the bus to college thinking it was over, loving how my life was, away from pornography. Then, all of sudden, that same evening, I was right back where I'd started.

It was a desperate situation. It didn't matter how hard I fought against it, how hard I prayed and begged God to break my chains, I always failed, always fell back.

We would do anything to escape this hook on our lives. The lads and I really did try it all. We would try to tire ourselves out so much during the day that by the time it was evening (when most of us were tempted) we were so tired that we wouldn't be interested in pornography. We discussed taping our hands to our beds at night or taking our phones off one another. Those of us who had sisters considered asking if we could share rooms with them. We even sent gross images to each other to see if we could put each other off the human body and, oh yeah, what's that Bible verse about gouging out your eye if it causes you to sin?[1] (Don't go down that road by the way. Praise God we put an end to that one quickly!)

And yet all our human efforts left us all still addicted to pornography. Eventually, I was done with it all; I couldn't take it anymore. I could not stand to be addicted to pornography any longer. Shattered, confused, angry, helpless, feeling dirty, forsaken, lonely and at the furthest point from God possible, I gave it all up into His hands. I cried out to a Saviour as my last plan of action.

I'm not sure why I thought this was a good idea, but I asked God to take me through all of 2017 without viewing

---

1. Matthew 5:29.

any form of pornography, and without the need for masturbation. In this year I asked for the true freedom that I now know only Jesus could offer me. Nothing I had done was working; my own grit and determination had not worked so far. If I was going to get out of this mess the answer had to be Jesus.

I dragged a friend into my mad prayer and I remember being at his house on New Year's Eve when Big Ben chimed midnight to mark the end of 2016 and the beginning of 2017. As we watched the London fireworks go off, we started our year of no pornography or masturbation.

It sucks at first, believe me. It felt like we had prayed a stupid and unrealistic prayer, but by day fifty we were both still going strong. Sadly, soon after day fifty my friend fell back into pornography and is still battling his way out. Now, that doesn't mean that God ignored him. It was my prayer; I had just got my friend to join me in it. Jesus frees people at different times and in different ways, and often it takes time and commitment. My friend will find his freedom; it just seems that this was not the way God had intended it to be for him.

I kept going. In the hands of God and with His leadership, and with the love and support of friends, I continued with this pornography-free year. The most challenging time was towards the end. The times I nearly gave up are too many to count. I would find myself burning with temptation, lying on my bed, sweating, unable to sleep, pushing through the pain and agony, fighting the call to look at pornography and masturbate. I experienced temptation to an extremity I never knew existed.

I used to call out to God a lot and say, "Lord, why don't you just set me free now?" God would tell me in my heart,

"If you finish this year you've started, then you've shown me that you do truly want to be free from pornography. So, when the year is up, if you've made it, I'll set you free."

With the help of my friends, what God taught me throughout 2017, and by His strength, when the fireworks went up to mark the start of 2018, He had led me through a year of no pornography or masturbation. At eighteen years old, six years after I had first become addicted to porn, God broke my chains and set me free! I have remained free and clean from pornography and masturbation since that day. I believe God will do the same for you if you will let him; He will work in your life, perhaps through this book, towards your own sweet day of freedom!

What's your story?

If you're reading this book because you too may find yourself controlled by this addiction, tell your own story. Those of us who have used or still use pornography find ourselves in that situation through different means. Are you in this place by a complete accident? Perhaps you thought it was normal and now you find it has taken over your life?

Whatever your reasons for finding yourself here, write your own life journey with pornography and masturbation. Think about why you use porn. Is it for pleasure, curiosity, to release pain, or to find love? How long have you used it? How do you feel after you've used it? Why do you seek freedom?

It's good to be honest with yourself about this. Go back to the start, take another look at your past and current habits and don't hide from it. And one day, and I honestly believe this, you will re-read your story from a place of freedom.

Tell your own story . . .

Marriage

If you, your story and this addiction are caught up within a marriage, I suggest that you don't use this book as your only source of guidance. Pornography can have devastating effects in marriage and I do not feel it right to give advice on something I have not experienced myself. Although this book could be helpful in making those steps towards freedom, I strongly recommend finding a further source of guidance that deals more closely with pornography within marriage.

It's not that you're any further from freedom than single people, it's just that there's more to think about and be careful with. In a marriage you're not just one person; you're a husband or wife, possibly a parent, you hold together a home, and your spouse (and maybe others) depend on you. You can still find your freedom and God will still work miracles in your life. A friend of mine was married with two children and still God set him free in that situation. But get yourself invested in church life or weekly groups and surround yourself with people who are also married and hold a strong faith. Seek mentors in these people, or find Christian counselling and look for other materials that are better equipped to walk with you in your journey than I am.

Key points

o This book was written by a survivor of a pornography addiction.

o It doesn't matter how long you've been using pornography, or how trapped you feel; God is bigger!

o If you're married and struggling with pornography, seek further help!

Think deep!

Forget the former things; do not dwell on the past. See, I am doing a new thing! Now it springs up; do you not perceive it? I am making a way in the wilderness and streams in the wasteland.

(Isaiah 43:18-19)

If you were free from pornography, how do you think it would benefit your life?

My thoughts . . .

Make notes below about your thoughts and feelings, following your reading so far.

Honest answers

What does freedom from pornography look like to you?

When you can wake up, go about life, go to bed and repeat this daily without thinking lustfully and with no intention of doing so, then I believe you are free. When you look at people with the love God has for them rather than the way the flesh would, then you are free.

(Jake, 17)

From the moment the Holy Spirit flowed through me, I just knew I was free – I can't explain it, I just knew. That is not to say I shouldn't be careful – because if I'm not careful, then I could possibly fall back into it – but I know there is no reason why I should!

(Max, 20)

In practice, I think I knew I was free from porn when I realised I wasn't going to fix this by myself. When I realised that some of this addiction and desire was the result of more deeply rooted things, and started to deal with them, I felt freer and lighter. The final step was when the temptation was gone; when I could actively just say, 'You know what? I really don't want to do that.'

(Megane, 22)

I no longer have any need to view porn. Occasionally, when I am feeling low or stressed, it is still something that can cross my mind to do, but I am in a place now where I have power over those thoughts and all of the reasons for them. I don't want to watch it again and this outweighs any desire I have to do it. I am aware of the shift I have felt in wanting to treasure my purity for myself, my relationship with God and a potential future relationship.

(Sarah, 23)

Porn and Max

I was brought up as a Christian, and from a very young age, I loved God with all my heart and soul. If someone fell over in the playground I'd go over and pray for them. It came naturally; I believed God could heal them. Why wouldn't I?

However, when I was five years old, I made friends with Drake. We became close and would do everything together. He had a computer in his room and, when I slept over at his house, he used to show me loads of websites that he had discovered. We mostly gamed the night away and they were happy days.

One night he had a new website to show me; this one was different. It showed girls dressed strangely, doing things I had never seen before. I don't blame him for showing me; he'd been exposed to it himself by a different friend. Although I did not understand what I had been shown, I liked the way it made me feel; in my wide-eyed childhood innocence I was curious, and I soon became hooked (I was still five at this point). It was strange; I didn't really think it was wrong but, then again, I'd only ever take peeks at the website on my parents' laptop in dead secret.

Anyway, as years went by, I became increasingly pulled into this darkness, with every new exposure tightening the grip that pornography had on me. Every night and all day I would fantasise about sex, unrestricted for a good ten years. I think it's pretty safe to say I was uncontrollably addicted.

Although I didn't realise it at the time, using pornography and masturbating so intensely and for so long led me away from God to the point where my faith fizzled out. It also became a huge contributor to my depression and anxiety later on.

Now I firmly believe that if I was able to escape pornography, anyone can. My situation was so desperately bleak; I was broken beyond repair. God, however, being God, can work miracles; there is no limit or restriction to His love for you, or me, nor His ability to transform your life and my life.

So, what happened?

All this time I still went to church, though my faith was dead. One day, when I was about fifteen a new lad turned up, called Joe. We quickly hit it off and soon became best friends. He began to excite me about God again, and things started to look up.

After a year there was a talk for the youth, explaining to us why pornography was damaging. Finding myself shaken, I vowed to myself that I would stop.

It wasn't so easy, though. Even knowing all the theory of why it is bad, and having the conviction in my mind to stop, I was powerless in the iron grip of addiction. I used to be impressed if I passed a week without satisfying my desires.

Then, one beautiful day, after fifteen years of being an addict, five of those years spent battling it, I was in my room at university, in the heat of temptation, feeling weak, almost about to give in (after a good couple of months of restraint); it was a sad and sorry moment. Suddenly, I had a thought. I should pray! I never prayed during my temptation because I didn't want to associate God with pornography; that's just weird.

But I prayed. I prayed, 'Jesus, help me, I don't want to do this, but I'm weak. Help me!'

Then, this peace unravelled down my spine, kind of like a shiver, but it was calm and it flowed through my body. Immediately I knew I didn't have to go back to pornography. The chains had been cut; I WAS FREE!

Years on, I still haven't returned to pornography and I feel great. I'm so much more at peace. My anxiety and depression have fizzled out. I don't objectify girls, and my faith is at an all-time high. This is not at all to say that I haven't seen temptation again; I have. Now, as soon as I recognise it, I fearfully run to Jesus in prayer and He gives me the strength I need.

So, you see, if I can escape pornography, you can too!

Max's story is amazing. Max is a friend of mine whom I've known for years. We grew up in the same village and went to the same primary school, church and youth groups. When I heard his story, I was blown away. It's crazy to think that from the age of five to university Max was battling with a pornography addiction. But then one day he prayed and he was set free. How cool is that! He spent years and years addicted and then in a split-second prayer he's free and has the strength to ignore any moments of temptation he ever faces. Wow!

I hope Max's story has shown you that no matter how far gone you feel, you can still find freedom in Christ. The truth is, though, Max is a rare case. His freedom story is rare. I've spoken with loads of people about pornography, and heard countless stories. Max is the only person I have met and known whose pornography battle ended with a single prayer.

I've prayed hundreds of times for freedom. All my other friends have prayed hundreds of times too. And yet, even with our prayers for freedom it was still years before freedom came our way, and for some people, they're still waiting.

So, what's my point? Well, I would love to say that all you need to do is pray now and you'll be set free. Definitely try it because for some people that's how it will be. But maybe you just tried praying and you don't think it worked, or you've already been praying and yet you're still suffering with this addiction. That's OK! Welcome to the club! Don't get disheartened or feel rejected if you've tried praying and God didn't answer your prayer in that moment. That's what the rest of the book is for, and you'll find other stories to come of people just like you and me. Try praying, and if you don't find immediate freedom, don't worry, just keep reading.

The Road to Freedom

It can be a tough journey, but we can learn ways to help us get there

Now for the part you've probably been waiting for: what you could do to begin this fight against a porn addiction. The rest of the book is going to lay out some practical things you can do, and some important truths you need to know to help you stand strong. Now, I'm not Jesus. I'm actually pretty far from it. Nor am I the apostle Paul, a great theologian. I don't have a psychology degree; heck, I didn't even finish school! So, you could rightly question everything I've written in this book.

I'm just a normal guy who spent six years addicted to pornography. I surrendered my fight to the Lord and He took me on a wild journey to show me how to find freedom in Christ from porn. While I lack some qualifications to write a book like this, I do hold one quality that stands above all. I've lived this journey you're living. I've walked this path and carried this burden. What's more, everything I'm about to lay down I have put into practice, mastered and committed to and I stand as living proof that they work – or at least, they worked for me, and perhaps this book will find someone out there who will find that it works for them.

But you're on your own journey. You know yourself better than anyone else when it comes to this stuff. You know your turn ons and your turn offs. You know when you're most likely to get tempted, and you know when you definitely will not fall into temptation. You know what kind of porn you watch, and you know what kind of porn you'll never go near. You know your reasons for ending up in this fight, and you know deep down if you do truly want to be free.

As a result, you may have picked up your own ways to avoid, fight and deal with temptation, porn and masturbation. I don't hold the key of all knowledge about how to get free. It's probable that there are many roads the Lord could take us to freedom, so if something works for you, keep doing it. Write it down so you don't forget, too! This is your journey and your battle, but if this book throws out a few new ideas you haven't tried yet, then great! But that doesn't mean what you're doing is wrong. Recognise your own ways you fight this addiction, write them down, and keep doing them.

How have you been fighting . . .

Expose It

Talking about porn is hard, but that's exactly what we have to do

Talking about porn is embarrassing; even just mentioning the word 'masturbation' is awkward. But this is one of the most powerful ways to face up to a porn addiction. If you can, tell someone that you are struggling with porn and find someone to keep you accountable in this fight you're in. It may seem challenging and, honestly, it probably will be, but you need to find someone you trust, and tell them anyway. Accountability is vital in this journey. You don't want to be alone and isolated in this fight. It's better to share the burden with someone else and get encouragement and guidance from an actual person, not just a book.

What is accountability?

Did you ever know someone who you could just say anything to? Someone who is there for you, no matter what? Someone you would drop everything for? It doesn't matter the time of day or the situation; you have their back and they have yours. The type of person who you could seek the truth from about yourself. Someone who is really honest with you and not afraid to say to your face what needs to be said, good or bad, but even through that, your bond is never broken.

You have a strong bond with these types of people, a brotherhood perhaps. Another way I would describe accountability is 'brotherhood' (or 'sisterhood'). It's people coming together, sharing or supporting the same goal and desire for someone else or each other. A strong connection and trust that can't be broken, even by painful honesty.

In terms of a porn addiction, accountability looks like having someone you can always go to when you're feeling down, when you need encouragement, or when you're feeling tempted, or you messed up. It's having someone who will check in on you, send you scripture, pray for you and ask how you're doing. Accountability is a lifeline, an extra pair of hands to help you out of the pit of addiction. Someone you can be really honest with. Someone you have that unfailing brotherhood bond with.

Ecclesiastes 4:10-12 sums up accountability, or brotherhood, perfectly:

> *If either of them falls down, one can help the other up. But pity anyone who falls and has no one to help them up. Also, if two lie down together, they will keep warm. But how can one keep warm alone? Though one may be overpowered, two can defend themselves. A cord of three strands is not quickly broken.*

Growing up I spent most of my time outside, with my mates. Thankfully my dad has always had the attitude that the garden is a place for mad fun and enjoyment, so he wasn't opposed to my mates and I wrecking the grass to build an assault course when we were about fifteen. We gathered together rope, tyres, tarpaulins, pallets and other scraps of wood we could find. We slung the ropes between trees, used the pallets to create walls to jump over, we dug the tyres into the ground to create tunnels and used the tarpaulin to create a watertight section so we could half-flood the tunnel. We would spend hours and hours just doing the course over and over again, getting more muddy, more wet, more tired, more cold and yet having the time of our lives.

On one occasion we flooded the tunnel completely. The tunnel got very muddy and dirty very quickly, and the ducks that my family kept used to make the water even more disgusting! As a result, you had to shut your eyes. So instead of making your own way down the tunnel at your own speed with your own determination and effort, we had to rely on each other. Instead of crawling down the tunnel, we would stretch one arm right out in front of us and enter into the water. The hope was that as you waited in the water your mate would reach you from the other end and drag you out.

This is like porn and accountability. If you go down that flooded, dark, muddy, duck poo-filled tunnel alone you will soon run out air, get disorientated, panic, or freeze up. If you have someone with you, someone who knows the truth, someone who cares for you and wants the best for you, then they can help drag you out. But if they don't know you're in there, how will they know to reach their arm inside the water and find you?

Why is accountability important?

I can't speak for the world here. Nor can I answer this question from the perspective of every issue, addiction or pain that people may go through. I can tell you, though, why accountability secured my feet in place as I stood before my own porn addiction.

When I learned to open up to one friend at a time, for the first time in my life, I felt and I knew that I was not alone. I used to have low moments where I would sit in my room, or lie on my bed, and think of all my Christian friends one by one and say to myself, 'They're not addicted to porn. They wouldn't drop down to that level. Yet, I am.' Even though God didn't see me like this, I had these feelings that I was some lowly Christian. I was a fake. How could I stand and raise my arms in worship alongside others who surely weren't like me? God didn't love me as much he loved my non-porn-addict friends. They were going to go on and change the world, preach the gospel and serve the Lord in mighty ways, while I would remain addicted to porn because I honestly could not see how I was going to get out of this one.

Then that all changed. I learned that nearly every single one of my friends was also addicted to porn. I wasn't some fake Christian. I was just like them. I was tangled in the same web; however, no one had shouted for help so I didn't know anyone was around me.

Once I had opened up, once my defences were down and I spilled the truth, then my healing began. In my friends I found a deeper friendship. I found someone to talk to. I found people cheering me on. I found honesty. I found people who wouldn't judge me when I messed up. I found people who were praying for me, calling me and being open about their journey too. I didn't want to mess up because I didn't want to let them down, and I had people to go to as a last-minute bail-out before giving into temptation. I found guidance on how to seek freedom and I felt closer to God. Most importantly for me, though, I like banter in the tough times. I like cracking jokes about the painful and challenging moments we all face, as inappropriate as the jokes may be. I don't know if you've ever laughed over a porn addiction, but it turns out all the nitty-gritty bits of masturbation can be the source of great humour. If I were alone, I would have carried all of this addiction, continued to feel far from God, not known where to begin and forever have felt lowly and dirty. But instead, I found a bond in my friends, and we held each other up and dragged one another closer and closer to Jesus, which meant freedom. Accountability and letting people in is almost freedom in itself.

God used my friends to pull me through, and I hope he used me to pull them through too.

Who can keep you accountable?

It's clear that from my story, my friends, all of whom were addicted to porn, were the ones keeping me accountable. However, this is not a common law. It just so happened that I came from a church that had a large youth group and so my Christian friends seemed never-ending. I understand this is not true for everyone.

It doesn't matter who or how many people keep you accountable. They could be your best friend, your siblings, your parents, or an older, wiser person within the church. It just depends who you feel close to, which varies for everyone.

Whoever you choose, they have to have a secure faith in Jesus. Telling someone you're struggling with porn, and you're looking for someone to be your support who doesn't have a faith or doesn't believe porn is wrong is not going to be helpful. You can't have someone supporting you who doesn't believe any support is needed. I would also avoid trying to convince them otherwise. The last thing you want is a debate which could give them the opportunity to change how you feel.

It may be that you open up to someone and ask for support, and this results in them opening up as well; now you've both opened up to each other. This is totally fine! Support each other! However, it could still be good to find someone who isn't a porn user and stay accountable to them as well.

Some of you may be reading this and thinking, 'This all sounds wonderful, but I don't have any strong Christians in my life that I'm close to.' My question to you is: do you go to church? Do you go to a youth group? Do you go to a weekly Bible study? Are you invested in a home group? Are you in some sort of Christian bubble? These are the places where you'll find the Christians you'll want around you. It would be really good for you to go seeking these places and these people.

I was open with one person and that then led to me being open with many other people. Because of the common nature of this problem, it's almost a guarantee that some of your Christian friends are in a similar place to you. The more people you're open with, the more people there are who have a chance of freedom! If you have friends in your youth group, Christian Union or church, try to be open with them as well. The only reason I was open is because a friend who was also struggling asked me about porn. You could be the person who starts that conversation which leads to someone else's freedom. It just takes someone brave enough to open their mouth and start those powerful conversations. So, who else could you talk to?

How do you start a conversation?

If you've managed to persuade yourself that you are going to be open with someone and you do think it's going to be helpful, you may be thinking, 'How do I even start a conversation like this?' Great question! And there's no correct answer. The truth is, however you say it, the first time you open your mouth to talk about porn will probably be tough. That's why you've just got to do it. It also really doesn't matter how you do it, and you'll probably just fumble your way through it in the moment.

As you know, my friend just blurted out, 'What's your view on porn?' and the conversation flowed from there. I have also just gone for it and said, 'Mate, do you use porn?' and then followed that up with questions like, 'How do you feel about that in terms of your faith?', 'Do you think it's wrong?', 'Do you wish you could stop?'

If I was going to do it all again though, if I was going to be the first one to open my mouth and seek help, I'd probably say something along these lines: 'Hey, I've been wanting to talk to you because I've been struggling with something and I feel like you're the person I need to share this with. I've been struggling with a porn addiction and it's not something I can go through on my own anymore.'

Try not to overthink it, though, as that may not be helpful. It's hard to plan a conversation like this because you can't plan what the other person may say. You could always just wing it and see what comes out in the moment. If you know the person loves you, though, and has/will always be there for you, then no matter how the conversation goes, you'll be in safe hands.

Key points

o Find someone you trust; a Christian who is secure in their faith, and ask them to keep you accountable in your fight against porn.

Think deep!

How good and pleasant it is when God's people live together in unity!

(Psalm 133:1)

How do you feel about opening up to someone about porn and masturbation?

No matter how awkward or scary it may seem, do you see how it can be so powerful to share this burden with others, so they can help you carry it until God takes it from you entirely?

My thoughts . . .

Make notes below about your thoughts and feelings, following your reading so far.

Honest answers

What are your thoughts on accountability?

Having friends and a mentor that came alongside me was really powerful, because part of the power of porn is that it's hard to talk about; you can be made to feel trapped and alone in your little corner of shame. We had a code word for when we talked of masturbation and that meant that we could talk about it far more openly with each other, whenever we saw each other. This made it a little easier to share. Being frank about it with people you trust breaks a lot of porn's power.

(David, 19)

Living with your mentor has perks; it is extremely hard to keep things hidden for very long. At 1am on a work night, I told her that I struggled with a porn addiction. There was a response of: 'I already know.' Filled with shock and a different type of intimacy and sense of belonging, another layer of vulnerability unfolded. One evening, I told one of my best friends about my issue with porn. She was so understanding.

(Megane, 22)

Tell somebody! Shame is going to tell you to keep your mouth shut, hide what you are feeling and doing. When I am struggling, I go and talk to those keeping me accountable. I might call them or text them, or tell them after the event. Have people in your life who hold you accountable. Keep the number small; it could be just one, but I found it helpful having two. Not that I would message both of them if I was struggling, but so that it wasn't only one person's responsibility to remember to ask how I was doing with it, or to support me if they were going through stuff themselves.

(Sarah, 23)

Temptation

We throw this word around a lot, but do we understand it?

Temptation. It's one of those Christian words. We chuck it about a lot, casually drop it into our sentences, sermons and conversations. I've done that myself in this book; just chatted away about this obscure feeling we all get towards different things. But do we ever define it? Or carefully consider what it is, or what it means to us in our situation with porn?

What is temptation in our situation?

For some of you, temptation is that feeling you know all too well. But it's not good. It's hard to resist and has been leading you down roads you don't want to go. That burning, heated passion that calls out for porn. A feeling that is hungry, never satisfied and relentless. It controls your feelings, your thoughts and your actions. It's like a wave that builds in you, and it will keep building until it's so big it wipes you out and you feel like you're drowning in it. You're totally out of your depth, it's totally beyond your control. All you can do, time and time again, is to listen to that feeling that screams from deep within you. You wish it didn't, but it does and it feels like it will never end. It's exciting and enticing but at the same time you hate it. It's comforting and freeing but at the same time you know you're guilty. You don't want any more, but you must have more. It's not something you own, it's something that owns you. You are completely at the mercy of its sweet, irresistible dictatorship over your life.

This is the temptation I've been talking about. This is the temptation for porn, that feeling that you have to masturbate. This is what we're dealing with. This is the feeling of a porn addiction. This is temptation. This is our enemy, and this is our fight.

Temptation is a recurring constant in our lives as we suffer with a porn addiction. But we must muster up the courage, the skill, and look to the leadership of Christ to be able to face up to this army of temptation, and fight back. If we don't learn how to fight it, we will never win this battle.

Three important truths the Bible teaches us about temptation

1. In temptation, God will give you a way out

> *No temptation has overtaken you except what is common to mankind. And God is faithful; he will not let you be tempted beyond what you can bear. But when you are tempted, he will also provide a way out so that you can endure it.*
>
> (1 Corinthians 10:13)

I start with this verse because when I was deep in addiction, no other verse remained as true as this one did. This is the key Bible passage to remember! You can break free, and God will give you a way out in the moments of temptation, if you look for them and pursue them.

I have this amazing relationship with my friends where we don't really ever text or use social media to remain in contact. We could go for weeks without seeing each other or messaging; yet, always, when we see each other again, or we do decide to message, it's like we were never apart. Keeping in contact with each other via the phone is not something any of us have ever really done on a regular basis. However, every time I was lying in bed trying to sleep but couldn't, because the temptation to watch porn was gripping me, out of nowhere my phone would go crazy with messages.

There were times when friends were asleep and then suddenly, in the deepest moment of my temptation, they would wake and message me. My friends would suddenly be online and want to chat; random people that I hadn't spoken to in years would want to catch up and text me, even if it was late in the evening or the middle of the night. You could say this was all just a coincidence, but I tell you now, I would never receive texts until I was deep in temptation. If I made the decision to answer those messages it would distract me from the temptation and I could rise above it. God will give you a way out, you just have to look for it and go with it.

I've had conversations with people who said that every time they were trying to access online porn the Wi-Fi would crash, their phone would freeze up or dramatically lose power. Many of them felt this was God giving them a few extra seconds to really consider if they wanted to go through with it.

When I'm tempted I remember this verse [1 Corinthians 10:13]. The way out could just be that I think of the friends to whom I'm accountable and whom I don't want to let down. Sometimes when I am being tempted, I have second thoughts: 'Is this wrong? Should I stop now before this gets out of hand?' Even though I fail many times, there's always a little voice in my head questioning whether or not I should do it. Once, before I was about to access a site, it wouldn't load and it gave me time to really question what I was doing.

(David, 19)

Temptation is going to happen, and it's going to keep happening, but in those moments, pray, seek and search for the God-given way out.

2. We are weak against temptation, but God is strong

Watch and pray so that you will not fall into temptation. The spirit is willing, but the flesh is weak.

(Matthew 26:41)

Always be praying that you don't enter into temptation, and be alert to your feelings. You must pray and invite God into your temptation, before, during and after. Our flesh is weak; you can't do this on your own. You must have a leader bigger than human desires; you must have God.

3. Temptation is lying to us, and leads us to bad places

Blessed is the one who perseveres under trial because, having stood the test, that person will receive the crown of life that the Lord has promised to those who love him. When tempted, no one should say, 'God is tempting me.' For God cannot be tempted by evil, nor does he tempt anyone; but each person is tempted when they are dragged away by their own evil desire and enticed. Then,

after desire has conceived, it gives birth to sin;
and sin, when it is full-grown, gives birth to death.
Don't be deceived, my dear brothers and sisters.

(James 1:12-16)

Do not be deceived. Temptation will present to you reasons, feelings and your own desires to entice you into porn. But it's a trick, it's a lie. Porn is never as great as the temptation builds it up to be. These desires we have do not lead to satisfaction, happiness, or a greater life. The Bible says they are leading us down a sinful, life-sucking road. So, do not be deceived, remain steadfast. Porn is a liar.

Key points
- There are ways out of the temptation.
- We must learn how to stand up against the feelings of temptation.

Think deep!
And the God of all grace, who called you to his eternal glory in Christ, after you have suffered a little while, will himself restore you and make you strong, firm and steadfast.
(1 Peter 5:10)

Can you think of any times where you found a way out, or you noticed a way out during temptation?

How will you invite God into your moments of temptation?

Do you agree that using porn is never as great as the temptation tells you it will be? Do you believe that porn is leading you nowhere and will not benefit your life?

My thoughts . . .

Make notes below about your thoughts and feelings, following your reading so far.

Three ways to brave the wave

Temptation is like a wave; it comes and it goes. But don't let it drown you. Learn how to fight it.

1. God stuff

Yes, I know. It kind of cringes me out too. Of course, a book written by a Christian, for Christians, from a biblical perspective *has* to include 'God stuff'. I also have asked myself the question, 'Does praying really help me?' and 'Can I honestly be bothered to think about this Jesus guy while I'm lusting after sexual material like never before?'

Trust me. I get it. But I'm going to say it anyway because as 'classic Christian' as it might sound, it still works.

Above all else, when fighting a porn addiction, your greatest plan of action is to stay close to God and invest in your faith. Try to be disciplined and develop a prayer life and a devotional time; try to be invested in church life, fill your mind with sermons, worship and Scripture at any opportunity.

It would be really powerful for you if you managed to 'hang out' with God every day and present to Him all of this and all of who you are. Don't hide from Jesus; He already knows the fight you're in, so take this fight to Him. Pray for guidance, self-control, strength and deliverance. Tell God when you've messed up, and ask for forgiveness. Equally importantly, praise Him every time you manage to stand firm against temptation.

Freedom will not come through this book alone, nor will it come by your own grit and determination. Freedom is found in Jesus and only Jesus, and all are welcome to it.

If you're not sure where to begin with growing your faith and spending more time with God, here are a few small suggestions about where to start. You can grow and adapt this as much as you want, to fit with your lifestyle.

I think a great way to begin walking closer with God is by praying every day. What do you pray? Well, this is not a rule that you must follow, pray as you feel led, but if you don't know where you're being led, start by asking the Holy Spirit to fill you afresh and guide you through your day.

Pray for forgiveness also. We're always missing God's standard and I think we often mess up and don't even realise it (at least I'm sure I do), so ask for forgiveness.

Pray for your needs. What do you need today? Not greedy, earthly, selfish needs, but serious needs. Perhaps your car has broken down and you don't have the money to fix it, but having a car allows you to get to work. That's a need, and it's OK to ask for help from God. Or maybe you have an exam and you want God's peace in that situation; that too is a need you can ask God for.

Perhaps you could pray for someone else as well? As Christians we are a family, and it's so great to pray for each other, even if people don't know you're praying for them. I'd like to think there are people praying for me!

Thank God for whatever He's doing or done in your life. Literally thank God for anything! Sometimes I thank God for toothpaste! Isn't it cool that we have this stuff that keeps our teeth and gums healthy? I bet if we didn't have that, we'd be asking God for something to take the pain away from our sore gums and rotting teeth! You can thank God for anything.

Also, listen to God. So often we forget this; we just speak at God and yet we never give Him time to talk back. Prayer is a conversation – don't let it be a one-sided one.

I also try to read my Bible every day. Now, the truth is I actually struggle to read long sections of the Bible at once.

Have you ever met those people who'll just read books of the Bible in one go? I wish I could do that, but I can't. It doesn't actually matter how much of the Bible you read a day! There are no awards for it, so read however much you want/can. Just try to read it as often as you're able to. If we want to lean in closer to God, then we need to know what He's telling us. If you don't know where to begin, start with the New Testament Gospels: Matthew, Mark, Luke and John.

Do you have a time of the week where you are by yourself? Perhaps some free time; like you always drive somewhere, walk somewhere, or are home alone? This can be a great opportunity to stick on some worship music and just have that slot as a time of worship. You don't have to be lost in the worship with arms stretched to heaven, like a worship festival. It's fine to be doing something else, like driving or walking, but use that as a time for worship.

Finally, every week if you can, try to go to church or some sort of a church-related group. It's really good to have solid Christian people around us who we can talk with, learn with and worship with. We need this normally, but especially when we we're dealing with an addiction. We're not called to be the 'lone Christian'.

It doesn't matter how long you pray for. It doesn't matter if you read the whole Bible at once, or take years to finish it. It doesn't matter if you hang out with God in the morning or the evening, once a day for five minutes, or all day. My point is to simply seek out God and chat with Him. We need this always, but definitely when we're facing up against a porn addiction.

2. Safety in numbers

When that wave of temptation hits you, when you can't focus your mind on anything because all you can think about is that heated sensation as your desire for porn builds, the one thing you must never let yourself be is alone. Being alone means that you are now in a free, private space to use porn. Luke 4:13 says, 'When the devil had finished all this tempting, he left him until an opportune time.' When you're alone, that's an 'opportune time'! I know how challenging it is to do anything else but use porn when you're in that head space. But if you can, don't allow yourself to be alone. You can go about this in different ways.

Just simply not hanging in your room as often as possible allows little time to be alone. Being downstairs in the presence of friends and family exposes you and keeps you accountable, even if they don't know your reasons for not being in your room (they don't have to know).

If you find yourself alone every Friday night and you know that's an opportunity to use porn, start making plans for Friday nights. Or, if out of the blue your family go out, take the time to see a friend, or go for a run. Don't allow yourself to be isolated.

For others, you find an escape in porn when you're emotionally down. This, therefore, is a moment of vulnerability, or an 'opportune time'. My point still applies to you – don't be alone. While you're finding people to be around, or just watching TV with your siblings, allow for your deep emotions to lighten. See if you can talk your emotions through in person, or over the phone with someone. If you're alone while your emotions are running high and they're causing you to desire porn, you don't stand much of a chance. If you're not alone, you can deal with your emotions in a healthy way instead of using porn.

3. Do something!

The Bible says to 'Flee from sexual immorality' (1 Corinthians 6:18). This can be a spiritual and mental type of fleeing, but it's also a physical type of feeling; a 'get up and run'. Run in a direction that is away from the temptation.

If you're being pulled into temptation, don't just sit around moping in the heat of it, hoping it passes, but deep down knowing you're probably going to end up using porn. Just get out of the situation. Get out of the room, out of that place where you're facing the urge. If you have to, just run. Literally go for a run. Make a move; don't sit in the thickness, letting the wave build in you. Get up, make a move, do something else, be productive.

Honest answers

What helps you to overcome moments of temptation?

The most effective way is routine – reading the Bible in the morning, only listening to worship music and reading the Bible at night, as well as a good, thought-provoking book about Christianity – this way your mind is always focusing on God. If we know that there are things that will trigger us to think or act lustfully, then we must cut them off practically; if it is social media, unfollow or delete it; if it is stuff on TV, don't watch it, or shut your eyes if you know you will be led astray. Always go to God after sinning; our flesh will try to get us to stay away, but God is there with arms open, ready to receive us, comfort us and forgive us.

(Jake, 17)

The main thing I'd say to others struggling with this topic is to look to God, for deliverance from our sins comes from Him. I always found that when I was spending time in Scripture, praying and worshipping regularly, I would be tempted less; when that stopped, even for a short amount of time, it always ended the same way – with porn. Also being open with my friends and being accountable to them, asking them to pray for me and sharing our opinions has truly helped me during this time.

(David, 19)

Finding other things to occupy my time has helped me a lot. Finding ways to express myself creatively, through art and music, for example, is a great solution as it lets out emotions in a more productive way. Get out of the house more as well; make an effort to see friends and meet other people. A lot of the time, people turn to porn as they're looking for some sort of connection and it's easy to pretend that a connection can be made by watching a screen. Seeing friends and forming real connections with other people is good for bringing you back into reality, and forms much more rewarding connections.

(Alex, 19)

Don't believe the lies that say porn isn't that bad, or porn is OK. Once I was tempted so much, I convinced myself that God in fact wanted me to do it. This, of course, is utterly untrue. Now, as soon as I feel even the smallest bit of temptation, I run to Jesus in prayer and He's never let me down!

(Max, 20)

Having one person with whom you are super-honest, who won't judge but will just listen.

(Megane, 22)

Not putting myself into situations where I might be tempted to act out, like alone in my bedroom with the door shut and on my laptop. Instead, I would keep the door slightly open, as a preventative measure, or just work downstairs.

(Sarah, 23)

Porn and Jessie

I first realised that the internet held things like porn when a classmate showed me pictures on his phone, under the science desk. Having had no sex education I was curious about a lot of the things my peers were talking about at school, and after finding out that this stuff was all over the internet I went ahead and Googled all the things I wanted to know. Urban Dictionary became my best friend, and then Google images became a better friend, and then the GIF section of Google images, until finally pornographic videos. I was exploring a world I didn't understand because no one had taught me and I was, understandably, curious to know.

Porn wasn't just a way for me to explore and understand sex, it was a way to understand my feelings. I had these feelings that I didn't understand and when I watched porn . . . I finally understood that these feelings were sexual and when I watched porn [they] were satisfied.

As I got older, porn became a way of coping when I didn't feel wanted. Whenever I was hurt by a guy I'd turn back to porn, and I watched the kind of porn where girls are treated like slaves or were controlled by men. For some reason it made me feel like it was OK to be treated badly by guys in real life. It gave me a really low opinion of girls and made me think that I was just a body for sex. These feelings were reinforced by some of the guys who were showing interest in me. I used porn both as a crutch and as a way to satisfy me sexually. But the reality was that porn didn't actually make me feel good in the long run. It made me feel guilty. I continued using porn, though, until I realised I was trapped and I couldn't stop watching it.

By the time I got to eighteen I was tired of watching porn; it wasn't something I enjoyed and it just made me feel guilty every time. I hated myself for doing it but I wasn't making any effort to stop it. It was also still a secret that I'd not told anyone.

I remember being on a short-term mission trip for a week and one girl sharing her journey with porn. Her courage made me realise I probably needed to say something to someone to break the power that the secrecy was holding over my life. I didn't tell anyone for another year. However, when I did tell someone, nothing changed instantly. I kept watching porn until eventually I decided enough was enough and I wanted to stop properly. I recognised how porn was changing my heart and my attitudes. My relationships were falling apart and damaging me because I was so broken. I wanted out of the hold porn had on me and the way it would make me feel.

More than that, I'd come to realise that porn is a distorted version of sex. It was not how real people have sex, there was no relationship or love between the people in the video. It was simply a tool for instant gratification, a purely selfish thing. I wanted to stop being so selfish.

I told the people I was living with at the time that I would be leaving my phone downstairs so there was no temptation but also so I was accountable to them, and I gave them permission to challenge me if they saw my phone was no longer there. I'm sure there was probably some praying . . . over me because within two weeks I felt able to take my phone back upstairs.

Watching porn stopped for a few months until I got a little lax and I'd watch a video. I'd hate myself for that. I'd pray about it and a few more months would go by without watching anything. It continued on like that for a while, and each time I would simply pray that God would help me have self-control.

Porn affected how I viewed my worth . . . and impacted how I let myself be treated in relationships. I'm not saying I'm perfect now. I'm not saying it's easy to quit. It's a daily battle I face and a daily, even hourly, choice sometimes. But I have to choose God's best over my selfishness.

Starve It Out

Sex is everywhere, not just in porn

Someone once told me that simply not looking at porn would not be enough to stop me feeling the need to use porn. He told me that I had to 'starve it out'.

Trying to stay away from porn showed me how sexual triggers are absolutely everywhere, whether we like it or not. Society throws sex at us in magazines, on TV, in advertisements, in shop windows, movies, in what people wear and even in what jokes people make. Throughout the day, my mind could be conditioned and tempted into watching porn; a sexual tension could grow in me without me even being aware of it. We are surrounded by sexual triggers every day from all different kinds of places. These sexual images and stimulants will keep feeding us sexual desires which can land us back in porn.

When you are a porn user, something like an underwear model in a shop window doesn't seem that explicit, and we have become used to seeing these sorts of images. Porn offers us a lot more than just a model wearing a revealing outfit. But once porn is out of your life, something like an underwear model will then start feeding you sexual temptation. If you truly want to be free, you have to starve yourself of all sexual triggers.

You need to ignore every sexual image, poster, underwear model, social media model, Hollywood sex scene, or revealing outfit. I'm not saying you have to walk in town with your head down, stop watching movies, or delete social media; all you have to do is learn to avert your eyes. When you're scrolling through social media, don't stop and stare at that image, pass it by quickly and ignore it. Don't have another glance at that poster, or focus on the sex scenes, or take a second look at that image on the side of the bus. That said, if you do find yourself looking, whether by accident, out of habit, or just because it's in your vision, bounce your eyes away and don't look again.

None of this imagery is as explicit as porn, but it's still feeding you and tempting you. Don't get me wrong, it's going to be challenging; we've grown up in a world where sex is casual. As a result, to overcome a porn addiction takes more than just overcoming porn itself; you have to overcome the sex that surrounds us in everyday life. I found that, after a time, it all becomes natural. Turning away from the advertisement, scrolling past that beach photoshoot, or getting up to grab a snack during the sex scene just becomes a natural response.

This might sound quite childish and another 'classic Christian' thing and in a way, it kind of is. But a porn addiction is hungry. If you starve it only of porn, it will feed off these other triggers that are around us in normal day-to-day life. If you allow yourself to focus on sexual or revealing images, pictures or people, it can so easily trigger you to go back to porn.

Even now that I'm free I still have this mentality. I've come from such a dark place and I can tell you that I'm never going back. I hated being addicted to porn. And I don't want to give anything the room to push me back into that pit.

A porn addiction is hungry; starve it dead.

Key points

o Don't let yourself get sucked into the sex that surrounds us daily.

o Learn to avert your eyes so you're not constantly being fed with sexual desires from the world around you.

Think deep!

Set your minds
on things above,
not on earthly things.

(Colossians 3:2)

What are the ways you're still being fed with sexual desires? How are you going to change that and cut them from your life?

My thoughts . . .

Make notes below about your thoughts and feelings, following your reading so far.

Honest answers

What damage do you know pornography has had on you?

At times pornography has affected the way I look at girls at school, mixing my thoughts with what I have seen in porn; imprinting this on them is so damaging and destructive both for me and them, even though they are unaware – this can then affect my relationships with them, as I can never look at them the same way again.

(Jake, 17)

It fed an addiction to masturbation and encouraged a lot of lust in my heart. It also created an area of my life which is separate and hidden from everything else, making me feel like a hypocrite in my faith, for being stuck in something that I know doesn't build me up or honour God.

(David, 19)

It has been a real struggle, as it is the one sin that makes me feel the most amount of guilt after having done it.

(Charlie, 19)

For me, I know it desensitises me, and makes sex too casual. Sex with another person is an incredible experience, embodying the love between two people, and strengthening the connection between them. Porn strips away all that connection and love with another person, instead connecting you to a screen. I've found that porn also makes me less productive, taking up time, and also diminishing my focus on other tasks.

(Alex, 19)

I have been healed from a lot of the injuries porn has caused me over time, but I did struggle with depression, anxiety and low self-esteem. Although most of my life I haven't been happy, lately [since being free] I've just had so much joy.

(Max, 20)

The damage that porn has done to me is the way it has cultivated lust in ways I didn't know were possible; lust in my relationships, in things, just a desire to have what I didn't have. It's also affected people around me. I told my parents and family when I was twenty that I struggled with porn and their reactions were fascinating. So supportive and understanding, but also sad because it was so much less than what God desired for me. Slowly, slowly, the images are being erased but still, every once in a while, an image of something I used to watch still pops into my mind and that's really rubbish! I have to ask God to keep renewing my mind and to remove this.

(Megane, 22)

Porn and Dave

All I remember is that I was still in primary school, because it was before I had a paper round and I used to pause and spend time in awe of the Page

3 girl; it was before I was able to steal adult magazines from the top shelf of a newsagent in my lunch breaks, working in a department store; it was before the internet, before digital, before mass distribution and availability.

Another boy at school excitedly told a few of us about an adult movie that he had; I can't even remember where he got it from but he had one, and I was ever inquisitive and always ready to bust any boundary that was put up before me. We must have all been coming into that place where girls were pretty amazing, mysterious and beautiful, and mainly unobtainable, because we were just silly boys.

I remember going to his house, and a few of us watching it not once, or twice, but about three times before his parents got home, because everyone's VHS video player was in the family sitting room. I can't even remember how I felt, but that was it, the first hook into 'adult entertainment'.

Hours, days, even weeks of my life were then wasted poring over pornographic material. The internet arrived and brought even more accessibility and availability; we no longer had to hang around a shop and find someone dumb enough to buy adult material for under-age kids. Images then turned into videos. It seemed that everyone you bumped into was into it, but even more hard core. Really, it was pretty normal.

However, inside me, the guilt raged like a furnace; the shame buried and consumed me.

From reading research over the years, joining accountability groups and prayer triplets, I discovered things and educated myself. Porn is like a drug.

I was praying and receiving prayer, holding my hand up. I was vulnerable, thought I'd beaten it, then I hadn't; I gave in completely, then felt filthy, dirty, hopeless and cried out to God to save me from this.

I remember having those awkward conversations with Dad when my parents found a magazine in my room, and all the things he said that were really wise and sensible; but it didn't help, not really. My brain had been wired from the age of eight.

Throughout all that time, I played in the worship band, I led worship, I led a small group, I led youth, I led a small church, I started a business, I got married and I had kids. Around me I had friends, youth workers, church leaders, family, all to whom I was 'accountable'. Some knew, some didn't, but few in my circle of Christian friends actually had the same struggle I did. Who wants to really tell anyone? It's pretty gross, and pretty embarrassing.

It was a long and painful journey. It's even more painful when you get married, then you have two beautiful little girls, and you realise marriage doesn't fix the problem. Great sex doesn't fix this. Now I was hurting those I love more than anything else in the whole world, again and again and again.

I was invited by a friend to sit in on an interview of a Christian author. I went because I felt obliged. I listened to his story, which was nothing like mine. Nonetheless, one thing did stand out for me: his behaviour patterns made him lead a double life and he destroyed his good life completely. While he was talking about that, I heard God's voice inside my head like a megaphone. 'If you don't stop what you are doing, this is what will happen to you.'

Instantly I knew what I had to do, without a doubt. I knew that I had to sit down with my wife and tell her everything; every little thing, every big thing, every horrible, evil and shameful thing I had ever done in the darkness and in secret that no one else knew about. She already knew a lot. We were the best of friends before we got married and she knew I was a work in progress. She knew a lot of my past mistakes, some of which directly impacted her. As I walked home, a lifetime of secrets and schemes filled my mind. This all has to come out, I thought; I knew it. So, I prepped her by saying, 'Tomorrow night I have to tell you everything.'

The next evening on the train home from work, I felt physically sick. Adrenaline filled my body. I couldn't sit down, I couldn't stand up. It was the longest journey home, ever.

That evening we sat together, and I talked and talked. I talked about secrets and sin and the shame that I'd been hiding for the last twenty years, and you know what? It didn't feel like a weight off my shoulders. It didn't feel so good to get it all out. It felt as though with every word and every story, I was physically slapping my wife in the face; it felt like emotional assault. Unfortunately, that one evening wasn't enough to get through everything. So, the next evening, we went through the process *all over again, until it was all out, everything. It still didn't feel good.*

I waited, knowing that I'd disclosed so much horror – from the thoughts in my head, to the physical acts that I had committed while married, and mostly while not married – and revealed the true nature of who I was. How could any spouse hear all that and not pick up the kids and leave?

Somehow, I always understood that I was forgiven by God. God is good. God is forgiving. But how can someone who has extended to you the trust and intimacy of mind, body, soul and spirit – someone with whom you have become one – forgive such actions done against them?

It was then that God blew my mind. Where I thought I knew how merciful He was, He showed me so much more. My wife forgave me.

I had made the choice to step out of the darkness and the lies, and stepped into the glorious light. The light was so brutal, everything was stripped away, but what was left was real, and God can work with real.

Practically, and from that day forward, it wasn't plain sailing, but the big hook no longer had any hold, rights or permission. We made a deal: I tell her everything I'm even thinking about. If I feel like I want to click on this link, or that image, or in my mind I want to escape, just for a minute, back into that old dark world, I tell her straight away before it can take hold. 'Temptation comes from our own desires, which entice us and drag us away. These desires give birth to sinful actions. And when sin

*is allowed to grow, it gives birth to death' (James
1:14-15,NLT).*

As a teenager, I couldn't wait to get married. I don't know
how many teenagers think about marriage but I thought
about it a lot. I was desperate for it. The reason I wanted
marriage so bad is because I naively thought that because
I could have sex when I was married, I would no longer
need porn. I also thought that by the time I was an adult,
this porn thing would have drifted away and out of my life.
I honestly thought that marriage and growing up was a fix
for a porn addiction.

Then I met Dave. I put Dave's story in my book because I
wanted to undo the lie that sex heals a porn addiction. Dave's
life journey taught me that I needed to ditch porn before I
was married, before I was older, before I had my own family,
because it turns out these do not fix an addiction.

Porn and Megane

*Do you know what is weird? I think I was already
addicted to the idea of sex long before I started
watching porn; let me explain why. When I was in
Year Two, I accidently discovered masturbation.
The understanding behind it, the 'whys' and 'how's'
were so far from my understanding of what was
going on. Yet, at the age of seven, there was clearly
something in my thinking that led to this sort of
acting out behaviour. Fast forward two years
and my friends and I had shared our stories of
masturbation. Get this in your mind, we weren't
even ten yet. Our understanding of sex was minimal*

to the extent that I still thought that if you wanted to have a baby, you needed to pray and God would place one in your belly. At this point I wasn't masturbating frequently; in fact, it only happened a few times a year.

Now, I can say that I think I was always fascinated by sexuality. Sex education lessons were completely fascinating and, to an extent, liberating because I could ask all my questions. Coming from a Christian background meant that sex was going to be talked about but definitely not at such a young age. Not to blame my parents, but it meant that unhealthy seeds around the topic of sex, lust, etc were planted. It was as if I was in the dark about sex and what God intended it to be.

In Year Nine, our family moved to Birmingham and, consequently, I had to move schools. Initially, I was really excited and ready for this move. Little did I know that this meant a move from a top-end single-sex school to a school with boys. They were so clued up on how sex and foreplay worked. Everyone seemed really experienced; everyone except me. I wanted to know how to make out with a boy when the time came; I didn't want Mr Future to think I didn't know what I was doing. So, I started to watch make-out videos on YouTube. The problem was that these simple make-out videos soon became boring and worked their way into being soft porn. Eventually, I typed into Google 'real sex'. The irony in that statement! I would watch it most nights before I went to sleep. At this point, I hadn't told anyone.

At fifteen, I had a boyfriend who was an atheist and, more importantly at the time, extremely experienced. He never pressured me but I was simply curious, especially now that I knew some of the lingo. We started having sex when I was sixteen. Bizarrely, it never felt like what the people looked like they were feeling in porn. I was still watching porn to feel fully satisfied. To be honest, it was as if my routine had complete control over me. He filled the romantic and intimate need, and porn filled the sensation tank.

I was still going to church, and I knew both of these things were not compatible with being a Christian; in fact, I had fully intended to wait until marriage to have any sort of sex. One Sunday, the youth had an open question pot where we could ask anything. I didn't have the guts to ask anything about porn, just in case they could trace my handwriting or recognise the piece of paper that I placed in the blue box. I asked a question about sex and, luckily, someone else mentioned porn. The youth leader directed that whole conversation towards the guys. I felt so excluded. At this point, shame came upon me like never before.

Eventually, after all the emotion of being in a relationship, my boyfriend and I broke up. Jesus had much more of my attention and I wanted to honour my relationship with Him.

Things only really started to turn around and change when I was in Year Thirteen. My best friend moved in with me for four months. We told each other everything; or so we thought. Three months into living together she said she had a secret that she had only ever told her boyfriend. We agreed that she would tell me, and I would tell her my deepest, darkest secret. Who would have thought that they would have turned out to be exactly the same! We both proceeded to try really hard to not watch it. We told some of our guy friends and they were so loving and supportive. We talked about the similarities and differences and then just prayed. Incredibly, I had a whole five months free from porn!

Half way through my Christian internship, I started watching it again. I was so annoyed with myself! Pretending to be a great Christian but actually living a complete lie. I yelled at God, 'Why haven't You healed me yet? Help me, please!' I really felt the nudge to look into the effects of watching porn. Discovering how much it affected my mind, heart and other relationships absolutely shocked me. This stopped me for a whole month.

At a summer camp where I was volunteering, I felt a nudge from God asking whether I was willing to share my story of porn with every person in that room. It turns out that you don't need to have already beaten your addiction to begin to feel freedom and reach people. It was as if my words of honesty and vulnerability were keys into other people's hearts. Within minutes, four people shared that they struggled with some sort of addiction. I wasn't free from it yet, but God was starting to bring freedom through it.

Still secretly struggling, I knew I had a passion from God to see a whole nation of girls free from this addiction, made aware of the impacts, being vulnerable and building kingdom together. As this passion was forming right in front of me, I could tell that it was becoming something exciting. I decided to tell my parents.

I told my mum in the middle of a coffee shop, right after I got home. In her grace she responded, rather than reacted, with the simply beautiful: 'Megane, you're being made new; you're white and pure and full of good fluffiness.' In other words: 'I'm choosing to trust Jesus in you, knowing that you are becoming more like Him.'

The hold the enemy had on me was growing weaker and weaker; I had finally got my fight on and was not going to let him win this battle. I had the sense that I needed to fast, and so decided to fast for seven meals. The number seven symbolises completeness which summed up what I gained from it. It was done. The battle was over. Although the habit of watching porn and masturbating is finished, the adventure of seeing God work through it constantly amazes me. I'm now married and able to make this journey with my husband.

Stolen Value

We are not an addiction

Know your identity

We are not an addiction. Whatever you may feel about yourself, you are not the addiction you are fighting. Your identity is not as a porn addict. God does not view you as that.

When I was a porn addict, I wasn't 'Henry the porn addict', I was just Henry. I mean, don't get me wrong, I'm not going to hide from the past or sugar coat the truth; I'm not about that. Sure, I was addicted to porn for six years. That's not a joke or a made-up story. I have viewed many hours of porn and masturbated to it as well. That's the truth and that's what I was doing. I never wanted it, but there you go, it happened. But still, I was not 'Henry the porn addict'. Those who knew about my biggest secret never saw me like that, either. Just like I didn't see my friends as porn addicts. They were my friends; it just so happened they were struggling with this addiction. I didn't love them any less because of their failures. They were still my friends and we would hang out as normal friends. Being porn addicts was never our identity.

If you're struggling with porn, this is something you need to understand. It's the most important truth. Being addicted to porn makes us feel dirty, a liar in our faith, and definitely not worthy of a Saviour. We feel less than others and wish we were better people. We're porn addicts, right? We're not worthy of love, church, or a relationship with

God. We can't tell anyone about who we really are. We'll be judged, looked down on and probably kicked out of the youth group. How can we stand before the King of kings and expect nothing but judgement from all of heaven and earth? We're porn addicts, and that's what porn addicts deserve, right?

It's all lies, though. God knew that one day His kids were going to get caught in something that was bigger than them and they wouldn't know how to escape. So, He sent His Son to earth to rescue them. Jesus came for people just like you and me. Jesus came for the porn addicts, and church is supposed to be a hospital for broken people just like us.

Have you ever read the Bible account in John 11:1-44 of Jesus raising Lazarus from the dead? It's one of my favourites.

There's this guy called Lazarus and he dies and is buried in a tomb. Four days later, Jesus arrives. After ordering the stone that was over the entrance of the tomb to be rolled away Jesus begins, in my opinion, the most powerful moment of his ministry. Even though Lazarus is long dead, Jesus says:

> *Lazarus, come out!* (John 11:43)

The account continues on, saying, 'The dead man came out, his hands and feet wrapped with strips of linen, and a cloth round his face' (John 11:44a).

Then what Jesus says to those at the scene is one of my favourite lines of His:

> *Take off the grave clothes and let him go.*
> (John 11:44b)

Jesus came for people like us. He came for the porn addicts, to rescue us, restore us and free us. Jesus does not watch us failing time and time again and look at us in disgust. He understands we're tangled in a web that we can't get out of on our own. He wants to pull us out of our tomb and take off the grave clothes, take off the lies and the shame that this addiction wraps us up in, and wants to watch us walk into His freedom. You are not a porn addict, you are you, and exactly the type of person Jesus came to find. You have great value in the eyes of the Lord, even when dealing with a porn addiction, because He sees beyond the addiction. You are His goal and His treasure. It may seem too late for you, but it's never too late for the Lord. He raised Lazarus back to life after four days of death. It's never too late. He's on His way to get you and one of these days the Lord will speak those mighty words into your tomb of addiction and say, '[insert your name] Come out!'

Know your potential

As Christians we all have a mission. In Matthew 28:19 Jesus tells us: 'Therefore go and make disciples of all nations, baptising them in the name of the Father and of the Son and of the Holy Spirit,'. Jesus also says in John 13:34, '"A new command I give you: love one another. As I have loved you, so you must love one another."' And finally, in Matthew 6:33 we're taught to 'seek first his kingdom'.

We're all called to do the work of God in different situations, places and in different ways, and no one way is greater than another.

So often when we fail God and miss His standards, we can feel like we can't be used by Him. When I was dealing with a porn addiction, I felt like God could not use me as I was such a disgrace to His name and kingdom. The truth is, though, everyone will fall short of God's standard.[2] Even the biggest, best and most famous pastors will miss it. Just because we're falling short by using porn, it does not exclude us from being used by God, and it does not mean God doesn't have a plan for our lives.

When I was fifteen years old, God met with me and told me that he had a specific purpose for my life. That's a very Christian way of saying God had a job that needed doing, and He wanted me to do it. I was fifteen, I was deep in a porn addiction, yet God still decided that He would use me and tell me that He wanted to use me, even though I was falling so very short of His standards.

It doesn't mean that we should just give up. Just because we still have value and purpose as porn addicts doesn't mean we should give up fighting our addiction. Porn is still short of God's standards, and if we do truly love Him we should want to live a life that's a life He would want us to live, and we should trust that He knows what is best for us. It's also damaging us. It changes the way we view other people and understand sex and relationships, as well as controlling us and trapping us in something that we can't walk away from if we ever wanted to. Porn is dangerous and naturally we should not want to be involved in it anyway.

Know your potential. We are all called to do the work of God in different ways. Being a porn addict does not mean you are any less wanted, needed or valued in being able to do God's work. God will still use you, and He still loves you, but don't give up the fight either.

---

2. See Romans 3:23.

Key points
- o Your identity is not as a porn addict!
- o You can still be used by God!.

Think deep!

I will be a Father to you,
and you will be my
sons and daughters,
says the Lord Almighty.
(2 Corinthians 6:18)

Do you want to be used by God?

Is there anything you feel like God is asking you to do for Him, but you feel like you can't because you're failing by using porn? Are you going to ignore the lies and let God work through you?

My thoughts . . .

Make notes below about your thoughts and feelings, following your reading so far.

Porn and Sarah

I feel ashamed to put my pornography and masturbation testimony into words; firstly, because I am a woman and, from my experience, it isn't as socially acceptable for us; secondly, because I am a Christian. When I was a teenager at a Christian camp, the boys and girls would be split up; the boys would have a talk about masturbation and pornography and the girls would be spoken to about body image and self-confidence. I learned very quickly that sexual temptation was something that, within the church, only men were expected to struggle with as they statistically had a higher sex drive, and women were not supposed to. However, my relationship with masturbation and pornography started much earlier than youth group talks.

I was first introduced to pornography through a female friend when I was in primary school. At the time I was shocked and horrified at what I saw, but also intrigued by what it was. Despite us only watching one video, it was enough for me to interpret that women got the attention of men and were desired when they exposed their bodies. Despite my 'female body' being nowhere near developed yet, my mind had been impacted by what I had seen and I started believing lies about where my value as a woman came from.

After coming across pornography videos years later, on our family computer when I was in secondary school, I was aware that I was enjoying watching them. It started off that I would watch a video every few weeks when I was home alone and procrastinating about working, but quickly developed into it becoming more regular. I did not have to watch very long into the video before feeling aroused and masturbating.

I soon realised that my dad had a pornography addiction too, and lied about it when asked, so I too decided that this was not something I would be honest about. Despite finding it difficult knowing my dad was watching pornography, I also took comfort from that fact that it was not just me who was struggling.

Watching pornography and masturbating became something that I would come back to when I was feeling overwhelmed, hurt and/or stressed. I would do it for a few days, weeks or months at a time, but then once the stress had gone away, or the hurt had been suppressed, I would not watch any pornography for months, even years.

I went to university and, at the time, was not struggling with watching pornography, as I was really happy. However, I quickly developed a relationship with a non-Christian who was regularly watching pornography. I felt pressure to fulfil the desires he felt myself, so we crossed boundaries physically. I asked him to stop watching pornography, as it made me feel hurt that he was seeking to feed his needs from others, virtually. That meant I then felt pressured to go even further physically to match what he had been watching online. After that relationship ended, I returned to watching pornography and masturbating to bring me comfort for a while.

I know that porn has impacted the way that I viewed myself in relationships. I used physical connection as a way of reconnecting when I felt insecure about myself or our relationship, as that is how I believed men would want me the most. It also meant that when we were being intimate with each other I was struggling to avoid going further than I had wanted. Porn desensitised my brain; in the heat of the moment I ended up engaging in some physical aspects of a relationship that I had wanted to save until marriage, which I have always regretted.

Remember

Before I bring this book to a close, I thought it may be helpful to condense it all down into five key points that are easy to remember. You may find it helpful to take a picture of this page or to cut it out and stick it somewhere you will see regularly. This way, once you've read the book, you'll always have a quick reminder about what you might find helpful in your journey.

- You're not the only one struggling, even if no one is talking about it.
- Check out 'Three ways to brave the wave' (page 51) for some ideas on how to deal with temptation.
- Avert your eyes and starve all sexual triggers out your life.
- Be open with someone, or multiple people, who will support you in your fight against porn and masturbation.
- Spend time with God.

.

The Power of a Pebble

Porn will lose

This is it now. This is where I leave you. I've given you everything I know about how to face up against a porn addiction. Hopefully you've learned something new, something you could put into practice to help you on your way.

For anyone who has read this book and porn isn't an issue for you, or perhaps porn hasn't completely taken over your life yet; for those of you who maybe only use porn every now and then but it's not yet an addiction – let me give you a piece of advice: Don't go there. If porn does not rule over your life yet, then don't let it, don't go down that road. It will very quickly spiral beyond your control and it will weigh you down every day of your life. It will mess with your mind in ways you won't even realise until it's too late. I don't tell you that from a holy throne of perfection. I tell you that because I went there myself and I sat in that pit of darkness for six years. All I wanted in those days was to go back in time to the age of twelve and not allow myself to look at that first pornographic material which opened the door to something I should have always kept shut. If you're still in control, then close the door and never open it again. Trust me. And trust everyone who you find in this book. You don't want to enter the world of porn.

For those of you who have read this book and you're already addicted, for those of you who opened the door to the world of porn and now can't find the exit, let me tell you something I wish someone had told me. It doesn't matter how deep you've gone, how far you went, or how long you've been running with porn, you are never too far gone for the Saviour of the world. I know it can feel like that. And I know the feeling of the years just going by without any change in your addiction. But you can be saved by Jesus. I don't tell you that from a wise, theological understanding of Scripture. I tell you that because the Saviour of the world reached into my pit of darkness and dragged me out. If He did that for me, then He can do it for you, because I am no more worthy of that than you are.

David, a small, overlooked lad, stood up against Goliath the giant. He took a pebble to a sword fight, and won.[3] My prayer is that you read something in this book which was that little pebble you were looking for. A pebble is all you need, because God will guide its direction to knock the giant down. Pornography and masturbation are another Goliath. They're just the giant we're facing right now – and Goliath will fall!

Pick up your pebble. Find your war face. Let's do this!

---

3. See 1 Samuel 17.

Key points
o You can do this! Your freedom is coming! Never quit!

Think deep!

Finally, be strong in the Lord and in his mighty power. Put on the full armour of God, so that you can take your stand against the devil's schemes.

(Ephesians 6:10-11)

After reading this book, do you feel more prepared to fight against porn?

From the book, what do you think will help you most?

Are you going to take this fight seriously?

Will you keep fighting, no matter how long it takes, until God sets you free?

My thoughts . . .

Make notes below about your thoughts and feelings, following your reading so far.

My Plan

Make notes below about how you are going to tackle this addiction.

I will open up to:

```
_____

_____
```

I am most usually tempted when:

```



```

To distract myself and begin to break this habit of using porn, I will:

```



```

I will commit my difficult times to God; I will do this by:

I will avoid temptation from the world around me by:

The Bible verses that will help me are:

My motivation(s) for stopping is (are):